THE ORIGINS OF THE FIRST WORLD WAR

by

BERNADOTTE E. SCHMITT

M.A. (Oxon.), Ph.D., LL.D., Litt.D.

Andrew MacLeish Distinguished Service Professor Emeritus
of Modern History in the University of Chicago;
sometime United States Editor-in-Chief of
Documents on German Foreign Policy, 1918–1945

1958

Professor Schmitt died in March 1969. No attempt has been made to revise either his judgements or his bibliography. References to later work will easily be found.   7/72

THE ORIGINS OF THE FIRST WORLD WAR

THE FIRST WORLD WAR broke out suddenly and unexpectedly in midsummer 1914, following the murder of the Archduke Francis Ferdinand of Habsburg, heir to the throne of Austria-Hungary, at Sarayevo, in Bosnia, on 28 June. Since no war involving the European great powers with each other had occurred since 1871, the possibility of a general war seemed increasingly remote, at least to the man in the street. At the moment, the international atmosphere was calmer than it had been for some time, for while some Balkan problems were threatening to become difficult, there was nothing unusual about that, nothing so dangerous as the questions that had been settled peacefully in the winter of 1912–1913. Another crisis would, it was assumed, be resolved by another compromise. Statesmen everywhere professed their devotion to peace and more or less sincerely believed their professions. Only a few persons in any country were psychologically prepared for the catastrophe which in the last two weeks of July 1914 plunged Europe into war. To be sure, there were prophets who had made predictions in English, French, German, Italian and Russian of impending disaster, all written in the ten or fifteen years before 1914, but, truth to tell, they aroused little attention and only a handful of experts believed these Cassandras.

The belief was widespread, on the contrary, that modern governments were much too enlightened to go to war. A great sensation was produced in 1911 by a book called *The Great Illusion*, by Norman Angell, an American who had lived most of his life in Europe. Angell asserted bluntly that wars did not pay. He did not say, as was sometimes alleged, that for economic reasons governments would not go to war, but he put it to them that if they did, they would lose much more than they could gain, for the complicated mechanism of modern business would be thrown out of gear and economic ruin would result for the victors as well as for the vanquished. Angell's arguments were by no means universally accepted and more than one formal refutation was offered. Nevertheless, the view was often expressed that if governments did try to go to war, financiers would stop them; while still others, chiefly socialists, hoped that the workers would not respond to the order of mobilization. But when on 23 July Austria-Hungary, in a formidable note accused its small neighbour Serbia of responsibility for the death of the Archduke and made demands that seemed to portend military action, it was instantly recognized that here was no ordinary crisis which might be overcome by negotiation, but that the whole constellation of European power was at stake. Illusions vanished overnight, and millions who before Sarayevo had had no thought of war accepted it as something which could not be avoided.

Once the shock of war had been absorbed, men asked themselves how it had happened, both the intermediate antecedents and the underlying causes. A popular explanation was that the war had grown out of economic jealousies and rival imperialism. Cited in proof were the trade competition between Germany and Great Britain for a generation before 1914; the conflicting colonial ambitions of the European powers which had more than once led to the " brink " (to use the term adopted forty years later); and the intrigues of high finance for concessions in Asia, Africa and the Near East, concessions for loans, railways, canals and other profitable enterprises. This interpretation was automatic for socialists, who derived their ideas from Karl Marx, but it was not exclusive with them, for an English radical, H. N. Brailsford, on the very eve of the war published a well-known book entitled *The War of Steel and Gold*, which said much the same thing.

Economic interests and rivalries undoubtedly had much to do with poisoning international relations in the forty-three years from the Treaty of Frankfurt in 1871 to the outbreak of war in 1914. Thus, the Austro-Serbian dispute, which in 1914 was to provide the spark for the explosion, became serious only when Austria sought to control Serbia by means of " pig wars " and harsh commercial treaties. On the colonial side, there were sharp conflicts between Britain and Russia in

4

Persia and the Far East, between France and Italy in Tunisia, between France and Germany in Morocco, between France and Britain in Egypt and Siam, between Britain and Germany in South Africa. More than once war threatened to break out. Likewise, the most famous project of financial imperialism, the Bagdad railway, involved Britain, France, Germany and Russia in long years of bitter wrangling. These disputes about colonies and the competition for concessions had much to do with the building up of large navies by the western powers, for sea power seemed necessary to guard overseas interests.

Yet economic interests, in the ordinary sense of that term, had little to do, directly at least, with the outbreak of war in August 1914. The most conspicuous trade rivalry of the pre-war years, the competition between Britain and Germany, was ceasing to be a cause of tension because the two countries were developing their markets in different parts of the world, Britain more and more with its own Empire, Germany more and more on the continent of Europe. In July 1914 the loudest protests against war were made by the businessmen in Germany and Britain, who foresaw clearly what war would do to them.

On the colonial side, to the credit of much-abused secret diplomacy, the great powers succeeded in partitioning Africa without recourse to war. To be sure, the British fought the Boers in South Africa, and British, French, Germans and Italians fought native people in Africa, but they did not fight each other. In the spring of 1914 Britain and Germany, sixteen years after they had begun to negotiate, were ready to sign an agreement providing for the ultimate disposition of the Portuguese colonies. Also at this time the western powers arrived at a compromise respecting the Bagdad railway and had divided the Ottoman Empire in Asia into spheres of economic influence for the laudable purpose of avoiding war over the Ottoman succession. Thus by 1914 the economic rivalries that were so troublesome in the first decade of the century had been in large measure adjusted, and they played no part in the hectic negotiations that preceded the war. Finally, it is to be noted that in 1914 the ruling groups in European governments were not men who thought in terms of business and economic advantage. They were usually members of the hereditary aristocracy, who thought in terms of strategy and military power and national prestige and who, in the crisis of 1914, paid little heed to the wails of businessmen.

The primary cause of the war was the conflict between political frontiers and the distribution of peoples, the denial of what is commonly called the right of self-determination (although this term was not ordinarily used before 1914). In 1914, from the Rhine eastwards, political frontiers, as determined by the Congress of Vienna a century before and by the wars of the nineteenth century, everywhere cut across well-recognized lines of nationality. To begin with, Germany held Alsace-Lorraine, taken from France in 1871, where the majority of the population resented having been annexed to Germany, disliked German rule, and wished to return to France. Austria-Hungary contained eleven different racial groups, nine of which were kept in greater or less submission by a ruling clique of the other two (Germans, Magyars). In the Balkans, racial and political frontiers rarely coincided. Finally, the western portion of the Russian Empire was made up of non-Russian regions represented today by Finland, the Baltic States, and Poland. Poland was the most notorious case, for it was still divided between the Austrian, German and Russian empires which had partitioned it in the eighteenth century.

So Germany was faced with the problem of French, Danish and Polish minorities, and Austria-Hungary consisted chiefly of minorities. Some minorities were treated more harshly than others, but everywhere they were growing increasingly restless and demanding change. In some cases minorities were able to look across their own frontiers to free kinsmen who, it was hoped, would one day free them from the oppression (as they saw it) under which they suffered. The Yugoslavs in both Austria and Hungary, denied relief by their Habsburg rulers, turned for help to Serbia under King Peter Karageorgevich, and the Romanians of Transylvania, in south-eastern Hungary, gazed longingly across the Carpathians at independent Romania under its Hohenzollern king. Neither Yugoslavs nor Romanians had in the past been united, but if the nineteenth century had seen the unification of Italians and Germans, why should not the twentieth century witness the joining together of Yugoslavs or Romanians? The Poles, too, dreamed of reunion, even if before 1914 there seemed no prospect of it.

6

More than any other circumstance, this conflict between existing governments and their unhappy minorities was responsible for the catastrophe of 1914. Germany understood perfectly well that the annexation of Alsace-Lorraine could be maintained only by the sword, and France knew equally well that the provinces could be regained only by the sword. The multi-national Habsburg state depended more and more on force, less and less on the loyalty of its peoples. The partition of Poland was maintained only by force. Since the astonishing victories of Prussia in the wars against Denmark, Austria and France were attributed to its conscript armies, it was not surprising that the new German Empire established in 1871 continued to recruit its armies by universal service. Inevitably, Germany's neighbours adopted the same system. Not only that, but every increase in strength, every improvement in the weapons of war made by one country, had to be met by all. From 1872 to 1913, this rigorous competition in the building up of armies went on, every government spending as much money as it could persuade its people to pay or its national economy would support (Germany bore this cost easily, but for Italy the burden was ruinous), without, however, any corresponding increase in security being felt. In fact, the proportionate strength of the various armies was not greatly different in 1914 from what it had been in 1872, but the feeling of insecurity was much greater than it had been forty years earlier. The memoirs of General Ludendorff, the most famous German soldier of the war, are eloquent on this point.

Of course, disputed and unstable frontiers were not the exclusive reason for great armies. From time immemorial European governments had maintained armies, partly to keep order at home, partly for use in diplomatic bargaining, and sometimes for aggression and conquest; but certainly the determination of monarchs and governments to preserve their territories intact in the face of growing dissatisfaction with the *status quo*, made the competition in armaments more deadly than it had been in earlier generations.

It was because of the increasing feeling of insecurity that European governments, one after another, sought to strengthen their respective positions by concluding alliances with other governments having similar interests. Germany enjoys the doubtful honour of launching this system of alliances, as it does

7

in the matter of conscript armies, for it was Bismarck, the German chancellor, who in 1879 made an alliance with Austria-Hungary and in 1882 engineered a second alliance, the Triple Alliance between Germany, Austria-Hungary and Italy. These alliances marked a turning-point in the history of Europe. There had often been alliances in the past, but they were usually concluded for specific purposes and were dissolved when the aim was accomplished. These Bismarckian alliances were destined to be permanent, the Austro-German treaty lasting until it was dissolved by military defeat in October 1918, the Triple Alliance surviving until 1915. Since the principle and the practice of the balance of power were as old as European history, it was to be expected that sooner or later a counterpoise should be created to the Triple Alliance. Birmarck succeeded in staving this off by very clever diplomacy (first by a Three Emperors' League from 1881 to 1887 and then by a "reinsurance" treaty with Russia from 1887 to 1890) which kept France isolated; but after his fall in 1890, his complicated system was discarded by his successor, and in the early 'nineties a Franco-Russian alliance—which had been Bismarck's nightmare—came into being. One combination dominated the centre of Europe, the other possessed the periphery.

Both of these continental alliances were originally strictly defensive, providing for the maintenance of the *status quo* and for assistance only if one party were attacked. Gradually, however, each alliance was transformed. The Triple Alliance was modified to permit changes in the *status quo* in the Balkans, in Africa and even in Europe, for the Italo-German treaty signed in conjunction with the second treaty of the Alliance concluded in 1887 contained a promise by Germany to support, in certain conditions, Italian claims to Nice and Savoy (which had been ceded to France in 1860 as payment for French assistance in the war of unification). Likewise, the Franco-Russian alliance was modified in 1899 to provide for "the maintenance of the balance of power", the words being meant to take care of the situation which would arise when the Habsburg state went to pieces, as it was confidently expected to do when the Emperor Francis Joseph died. Finally, in 1909, the Austro-German alliance was given a new twist when the chief of the German general staff, by an exchange of letters

8

with his Austro-Hungarian opposite number, promised that if Austria invaded Serbia and in consequence Russia intervened on behalf of Serbia, Germany would go to the assistance of Austria-Hungary, a promise that Bismarck had consistently refused to give, for he insisted that Austria must not provoke Russia. Thus the alliances ceased to be the guarantors of the *status quo*, and might instead become instruments of aggression. The terms of the several treaties and commitments were not published, but each side came to suspect the other of sinister intentions.

Down to the turn of the century, Great Britain did not join either of the continental groups, preferring a policy of " splendid isolation ". The two groups, although directed against each other, were often more concerned, in the 'nineties, with diplomatic action against Great Britain, and stood, as it were, side by side, rather than face to face. In 1898 and again in 1901, Britain tried to come to an agreement with Germany, but the German terms proved too high: Britain was asked to join the Triple Alliance, which it was unwilling to do because it was reluctant to underwrite the shaky Habsburg state. The German chancellor of the day, Count Bülow, was sure that in the end Britain would come to heel and stood on his terms. When in 1904 Britain adjusted its many old disputes with France and in 1907 compromised its differences with Russia in the Middle East, Germany found itself confronted by a Triple Entente which had been deemed impossible. Europe was not mentioned in any of the several agreements, but the British, French and Russian governments were all suspicious of Germany, and by settling their own differences they ensured themselves free hands in dealing with Germany. Nevertheless, for years after the formation of the Entente, Germany held on to a policy based on the premiss of irreconcilable hostility between Britain and the Franco-Russian Alliance.

At the beginning of the twentieth century, Germany was the most restless nation in Europe. Its population, its industry, its foreign trade were growing more rapidly than those of any other country, and its future seemed brilliant, at least to other countries. But the Germans themselves were not so sure. As they looked at the world around them, they observed that Britain and France had secured control, in one form or another,

9

of the most desirable parts of Africa, held large possessions in Asia, and ruled the ocean lanes from innumerable islands in the seven seas, which provided naval bases and coaling stations. In comparison, the German colonies in Africa and Asia and the German islands in the Pacific were pitifully inadequate. Even the colonial nations of the past, Spain, Portugal, the Netherlands, were better off than Germany. In the current view colonial possessions were considered necessary for an industrial nation, in order to supply raw materials needed in industry and to furnish markets for manufactured goods and opportunities for the investment of capital, and Germany, not having rich, productive and populous colonies, felt discriminated against. So there arose a tremendous agitation and a loud cry for " a place in the sun ", and along with it, the charge was heard that Germany's rivals, principally Britain and France, were standing in the way of Germany's acquiring what was its just due. The Pan-German League, a small but noisy and influential association, proclaimed what needed to be done in Europe to achieve the unification of the German people, and innumerable books and pamphlets set forth in considerable detail what was wanted elsewhere in the world. Since these programmes were to be realized at the expense of other nations and the view was often expressed that if necessary Germany would use force to accomplish its ends, it was not surprising that the countries most affected should draw together, as Britain, France and Russia did in the Triple Entente.

The German government never associated itself with the specific demands of the expansionist agitation, but it resorted to methods of diplomacy which gave great offence. Thus, it took advantage of the Boer war in South Africa to force concessions from Britain in Samoa; it used the opportunity offered by the Russo-Japanese war to secure a tariff treaty from Russia that was unduly advantageous to Germany; and when Russia, France's ally, was being defeated in the Far East, Germany compelled France to get rid of its foreign minister and to change its policy in Morocco. The resistance which Britain, France and Russia offered to this policy, which they regarded as blackmail, was denounced by Germany as " encirclement ", and Germany reacted to it by giving unqualified support to the action of Austria-Hungary when that power proclaimed the annexation of Bosnia in 1908, which caused great irritation in Russia.

In addition, the German government, from 1900 onwards, began the construction of a navy which was intended to be second only to that of Great Britain. This was a pet project of the Emperor William II, and he declined all suggestions from Britain for a limitation of naval armaments. The faster the German fleet grew, the more alarmed the British became, the closer they drew to the French and the Russians—and the more the Germans complained of " encirclement ". As the years passed, the more clearly did Europe appear to be divided between the Triple Alliance and the Triple Entente.

Actually, things were not so simple. In 1902 Italy made a secret agreement with France by which it promised to remain neutral if France went to war with Germany in consequence of a German attack on Russia. In 1909 Italy concluded a secret agreement with Russia by which both parties recognized each other's interests in the Balkans and promised support for each other's policies. Thus the Triple Alliance was for some years a broken reed. But in the Balkan wars of 1912–1913 Italy worked with Austria-Hungary to establish an independent Albania, and in the winter of 1913–1914 negotiated new military and naval conventions with Germany and Austria-Hungary which seemed to bring the wavering ally back into the fold. The chief of the German general staff, General von Moltke, became convinced that Italy's loyalty was " not open to doubt " and he acted on that assumption in the crisis of July 1914.

The Triple Entente never became so closely-knit as the Triple Alliance, for the British government refused to commit itself to go to the help of France, in spite of French arguments that an Anglo-French alliance would be the most effective means of discouraging Germany from going to war. The most that Britain would concede was a promise, made in 1912, that if either Britain or France had grave reason to expect attack by a third party or a threat to the general peace, they would consult with each other and if they should decide to take common action, they would put into effect the plans which their general staffs had drawn up.

These plans, elaborated from 1906 on, provided for the sending of a British army of 160,000 troops to fight in France alongside the French army, and for the deploying of the French navy in the Mediterranean while the British fleet guarded the North Sea and the Channel. The French had to be satisfied (as of course they were not!) with this "half-alliance", which left the British free to decide whether to intervene—a freedom of which they took full advantage in 1914.

Anglo-Russian relations never reached the degree of intimacy of those between Britain and France. Russian interests in the Near East were not regarded in Britain as something Britain might have to fight for, and Russian activity in Persia was much disliked. In the spring of 1914 the Russian foreign minister, Sazonov, proposed that the Triple Entente should be converted into a Triple Alliance, but this was rejected by the British foreign secretary, Sir Edward Grey. Grey agreed, however, to the Russians being informed of the Anglo-French notes exchanged in 1912 and to the opening of conversations between the British and Russian admiralties, so that, as he said to the German ambassador, although Britain was not allied with France and Russia, it "did from time to time talk with them as intimately as allies".

Thus in July 1914 the two groups, Triple Alliance and Triple Entente, were at long last ranged face to face, three on each side. Was war the inevitable consequence of this schism of Europe? At the moment there was no immediate prospect of it. Relations between Britain and Germany had improved considerably since 1912. An informal agreement had been reached for the construction of battleships in the ratio of 16 : 10. During the crisis of the Balkan wars (1912–1913) Britain and Germany had co-operated to restrain Russia and Austria respectively, and in 1914 they had negotiated and were ready to sign two agreements regarding the future of the Portuguese colonies and settling their differences about the Bagdad railway. This led the British to expect that in the event of another Balkan crisis they could count on German help to deal with it; on the other hand, the Germans drew the conclusion that Britain would no longer necessarily take the side of France in the event of war.

After the great crises of 1905 and 1911 over Morocco, during which Germany seemed ready for war with France, the relations between those two countries had also taken a turn for the better. In February 1914 an agreement was reached concerning railway schemes and spheres of economic interest in Turkey, and the president of the Republic, Poincaré, who was later to be denounced as a warmonger, breaking a tradition of forty years, had dined at the German embassy. If Alsace-Lorraine had not been forgotten, there was practically no sentiment for a " war of revenge " (as the German ambassador recognized), and the elections of May 1914 gave a majority to the parties to the Left, who wished to abolish the three-years' military service restored in 1913.

In the midsummer of 1914, then, neither Anglo-German nor Franco-German relations involved any threat to peace. On the other hand, there was plenty of explosive material lying around in the Near East. At the end of 1913 such tension was produced between Russia and Germany by the despatch of a German military mission to Constantinople for the rehabilitation of the Turkish army that Sazonov toyed with the idea of seizing the Straits by force (an idea rejected by his colleagues and the Russian general staff); a compromise was patched up, but public opinion in both countries remained excited. Austria and Italy were intriguing against each other in Albania, Bulgaria was sullenly nursing its defeat the year before at the hands of Serbia, Greece and Romania, Greece and Turkey were at loggerheads about certain islands in the Ægean. As it happened, however, the spark that touched off the explosion was a completely unexpected incident, the murder of the Archduke Francis Ferdinand of Habsburg at Sarayevo on 28 June.

The tragedy at Sarayevo was the culmination of an antagonism between Austria-Hungary and Serbia that had been growing for a generation. In 1859 the Habsburgs had faced the question of Italian unification, and had been driven out of Italy: in 1866 they faced the same problem in Germany, and with the same result. From 1903, when the pro-Austrian king of Serbia, Alexander Obrenovich, was assassinated, they were confronted with the Yugoslav problem. At the beginning of the century, the Yugoslavs were widely disunited in Austria, Hungary, Bosnia, Serbia, Montenegro and Turkey. In the decade before 1914 it became evident that a national movement was gaining headway because of the rather shabby treatment of the Yugoslavs within the Habsburg monarchy, and one of two things seemed likely to happen: either Austria-Hungary must bring the Yugoslavs outside the Monarchy (those in Serbia, Montenegro and Turkey) under Habsburg rule, or the Serbs, the most energetic group among the Yugoslavs and the only one possessing an independent state, would detach their kinsmen from Habsburg rule and establish a unified independent Yugoslav state. If Habsburg experience with the Italians and the Germans provided any guide, the second contingency was the more likely.

Naturally the ruling groups in Austria-Hungary favoured the first course. The military party, led by the chief of the general staff, General Conrad von Hötzendorf, made no secret of its desire for war against Serbia, which would lead to direct annexation of the troublesome little neighbour. The political leadership was more cautious, thinking in terms of a customs union or a change of dynasty, which might be accomplished by diplomacy, but it was just as eager as the soldiers to put an end to Serbian independence and thus extinguish the restlessness of its Yugoslav peoples. The first step in this direction was the annexation of Bosnia-Herzegovina, two provinces with a mixed population of Serbs and Croats which had been under Habsburg administration since 1878 but were nominally still parts of the Ottoman Empire. This action precipitated a six months' crisis (October 1908–March 1909), which almost ended in an Austrian attack on Serbia and was settled only after Germany had sent a near-ultimatum to Russia requiring the cabinet of St. Petersburg to recognize the annexation without reference to a European conference. The Russian foreign minister of the time, Izvolsky, accused his Austro-Hungarian opposite number, Aehrenthal, of tricking him, and he bitterly resented the intervention of Germany at the last minute. The echoes of this conflict had not died away in 1914.

In the plans of the Austro-Hungarian government to deal with the Yugoslav problem, the Archduke Francis Ferdinand played a peculiar role. He had come to the conclusion that the existing Dual system, by which the Germans ruled in Austria, the Magyars in Hungary, although both were minorities, was driving the Monarchy to destruction, and he hated the Magyar clique and was determined to clip its power. He proposed to solve the Yugoslav problem by granting to the Yugoslavs within the Monarchy full autonomy (which would destroy the Dual system) and then bring Serbia into some kind of connection with the Monarchy. Whether Francis Ferdinand would have been able to accomplish this is anybody's guess. He was a rather hot-headed, bigoted, avaricious man who was heartily disliked by the great majority of his future subjects, and any attempt to carry out his plan, had he lived to succeed his uncle Francis Joseph, would have met with determined resistance by the Germans and Magyars. But his violent death at the hands of a man of Serbian race (who, however, was a Habsburg subject) provided the forward party with an excuse for action against Serbia that was too tempting to be neglected.

The full circumstances of the crime at Sarayevo have never been cleared up. That the conspirators were fitted out with arms in Belgrade and secretly passed across the frontier into Bosnia became known in 1914 and was used by the Austro-Hungarian government as justification for the demands made on Serbia. But precisely who inspired the crime,* how much the Serbian government knew about the plot in advance, what steps it took to prevent the crime's execution—either by warning Vienna or by attempting to stop the assassins from crossing into Bosnia, whether also the authorities in Sarayevo took proper precautions to protect the heir to the throne, are questions to which precise answers are still not possible. Actually the answers do not really matter, for an official sent from Vienna to Sarayevo reported that the responsibility of the Serbian government was not established; yet Austro-Hungarian policy could hardly have been more drastic if Serbian official complicity had been proved.

The situation in 1914 cannot, however, be judged exclusively in terms of Austro-Serbian relations, for Serbia, a small nation of 5,000,000 people, occupied a key position in Europe. Romania was the ally of Austria-Hungary; Bulgaria was anxious to be taken into the Triple Alliance; in Turkey German influence was stronger than that of any other power. If Serbia were brought under Austrian control, then German-Austrian influence would prevail from Berlin to Bagdad. If, on the other hand, Serbia were maintained as an independent state, a wedge would be driven into the German-Austrian-Turkish

* The person most often credited was the chief of the intelligence section of the Serbian general staff, Colonel Dragutin Dimitriyevich, but the evidence is not conclusive.

combination, and Constantinople would be susceptible to Russian, French and British pressure. So the crisis of July 1914 was concerned with more than the question whether, as Austria-Hungary demanded, Austrian officials should go into Serbia and investigate the *minutiæ* of the crime at Sarayevo. The fundamental issue was a test of strength between the Triple Alliance and the Triple Entente, the outcome of which would affect the balance of power in Europe for an incalculable time to come.

II

All the governments were responsible, in greater or less degree, for building up the system of alliances and for the great accumulation of armaments. To that extent they all contributed to the tension that came to a head in July 1914. But they were not equally responsible for the fatal turn of events, the course of which can be followed in microscopic detail. When the crisis culminated in war, the governments began to issue collections of diplomatic documents in coloured (White, Blue, Orange, Red, Yellow, Grey, from the colour of the cover) " Books ", in which each set forth its case and laid the blame for the war on the other side. Not only was it essential to convince its own people of the rightness of its conduct, but it was deemed equally important to gain the good will of neutrals, notably of the United States. For years endless debate raged throughout the world over this question of " war guilt "; a book by an eminent American lawyer, *The Evidence in the Case*, by James M. Beck, enjoyed a wide circulation. After the war, much fuller collections of documents were published which were selected by historians rather than by politicians and propagandists, and it became evident that the documents put out in 1914 had been chosen to prove a case and had often been " edited ", that is, tampered with; that awkward documents had been suppressed and still others invented. From the fairly complete diplomatic files available for July 1914, together with the memoirs of politicians, diplomatists and military men, a dispassionate and accurate account can now be written of the action of European diplomacy from the murder at Sarayevo on 28 June to the outbreak of the general European war in August.

The Austro-Hungarian government quickly decided that the heaven-sent opportunity for a reckoning with Serbia should not be lost. But since action against Serbia was likely to bring about the intervention of Russia, it was essential for the cabinet of Vienna to know what Germany would do in such a situation. To be sure, the German general staff had declared in 1909, during the Bosnian crisis, that Russian intervention on behalf of Serbia would cause Germany to mobilize, which, in German terminology, was the prelude to war. But, during the crisis of the Balkan wars of 1912–1913, the German government had consistently restrained the war party in Vienna, and furthermore, the German Emperor, William II, was supposed to entertain considerable partiality for Serbia. In order to discover the state of mind of Berlin, the Austro-Hungarian foreign minister, Count Berchtold, sent both an official note and a private emissary to the German capital; also Francis Joseph wrote a letter to William II. The letter stated that Austria-Hungary must aim at " the isolation and diminution of Serbia ", which must be " eliminated as a political factor in the Balkans ". The emissary, Berchtold's *chef de cabinet*, Count Hoyos, explained that the Austrian plan was to " march into Serbia " without any warning and to partition Serbia between the Monarchy, Albania and Bulgaria.

Only two weeks before, the German chancellor, Bethmann Hollweg, had said that in the event of a new crisis arising in the Balkans, " whether . . . it would come to a general European conflagration would depend exclusively on the attitude of Germany and England ". But when Hoyos appeared in the German capital on 5 July, this caution was laid aside. The Austrian plan to invade and partition Serbia was cordially received by the German Emperor and the German government, and immediate action was urged on the cabinet of Vienna. Because a royal personage had been murdered, William II professed to believe that Tsar Nicholas II would be loath to go to the help of Serbia, but if he did, Germany was ready to support its ally and to wage war against Russia and France. This decision was not a matter of Germany putting its head into a noose (as is sometimes asserted) and signing away its freedom of action; both emperor and government knew exactly what they were doing. They made their decision on the assumption that Great Britain would remain neutral (in spite of the fact that the German ambassador in London, Prince Lichnowsky, had been reporting for eighteen months that in the event of war between Germany and France, Britain would join France). The general staff was confident that Germany and Austria-Hungary could defeat Russia and France, and, assuming war to be inevitable, it now welcomed the prospect of war, for victory would be easier in 1914 than later, when French and Russian military plans would be nearer completion. Some conservative elements in Germany looked upon war as a good means of dealing with the menace of socialism, which seemed to be steadily increasing. The emperor and the chancellor took their decision without reference to the foreign minister, a cautious man who happened to be away on his honeymoon and who had hitherto worked to restrain Austria, and without any formal consultation of the highest authorities of the German Empire; furthermore, the decision was taken instantly, without reflection. William II and Bethmann accepted the risk of war with unbelievable nonchalance; it was they who put the system of European alliances to the test. Without this German action, it is unlikely that a European war would have broken out in the summer of 1914.

For twenty-odd years German policy had vacillated between East and West. From 1890 to 1914, that is, the period after the fall of Bismarck during which William II was the ruler of Germany, the German government pursued its policy of expansion in both directions. Admiral Tirpitz and the navy people thought Britain the enemy and concentrated on building a fleet, although the more they built the more they alarmed Britain. The general staff thought in terms of French enmity and demanded as much money as possible for the army. Business men were divided, some wishing to go into Africa, others into the Near East. Neither the emperor nor any of his chancellors could make up their minds where the fundamental interest of Germany lay; in one sense, they thought that Germany was strong enough to move in both directions. In 1914, however, they were seriously concerned about the stability of Austria-Hungary the one sure ally, and they persuaded themselves that only a successful military demonstration against Serbia could stop the process of Habsburg decay. The decision of July 1914 to support Austria-

Hungary against Russia, in the calculation that Britain would remain neutral, may be interpreted as meaning that the long indecision had, at least for the moment, been resolved by a decision to go East.

The Austro-Hungarian government could now act. But because of the opposition of the Hungarian premier, Count Tisza, the plan to " march into Serbia " without warning was abandoned. At a ministerial council held on 7 July, in its place a forty-eight hour ultimatum was decided upon which theoretically would provide Serbia with a chance to submit. Actually, seven supposedly unacceptable demands were included, in order to ensure the rejection of the ultimatum and thus pave the way for military action. In the minds of the Austro-Hungarian ministers the treatment to be meted out to Serbia after the war included " rectifications of frontier " for the benefit of the Monarchy, while other parts of its territory were to be apportioned to other Balkan states; what was left might be attached to the Monarchy by a military convention to be signed by a new dynasty. These designs were of course not mentioned when the Austro-Hungarian government assured the other powers that it did not intend to take Serbian territory for itself.

The ultimatum was presented to the Serbian government on 23 July. It contained ten demands, the most important of which required Serbia to admit Austrian officials into Serbia for the suppression of the agitation against the Monarchy and to take action against the persons involved in the murder of Sarayevo. Outside of Austria and Germany, the ultimatum was regarded as a monstrous document which no independent state could accept. To the intense surprise and annoyance of Vienna, the Serbian reply, delivered a few minutes before the expiry of the ultimatum on 25 July, was conciliatory and to a large extent appeared to accept the Austrian demands, as was later stated by both William II and Bethmann Hollweg. Nevertheless, diplomatic relations were broken off, partial mobilization of the Austrian army was ordered, and on 28 July war was declared against Serbia. The military chiefs would have preferred to wait until mobilization had been completed, but insistent German pressure forced immediate action, which began with the bombardment of the Serbian capital on 29 July.

This action precipitated the intervention of Russia. For generations the principal Russian interest in the Near East had been the question of the Straits: how to break through the barrier of the Bosphorus and the Dardanelles and secure free access to the Mediterranean for Russian merchantmen and men-of-war. Although various plans for accomplishing this had been devised since 1798, no plan existed in 1914, for the Russian generals had rejected a suggestion of the foreign minister for seizing the Straits. The other facet of Russia's Near Eastern policy was the defence of the Slav peoples of the Balkans against Turkish misrule or German pressure. Ever since the Bosnian crisis of 1908, Serbia had looked to Russia for help against Austrian action, but Russia was weak after the war against Japan and the abortive revolution of 1905, so successive foreign ministers kept putting off the importunate Serbs with promises for the future. The Russian government probably did not want war in 1914, for its army was still in process of reorganization and revolutionary symptoms were again in evidence, but, this time, it had to help Serbia or see that country be crushed by Austria. The German argument that the Austro-Serbian conflict could be "localized" was completely unrealistic, all the more so since the Austrian assurances of disinterestedness were equivocal. The Russian foreign minister, Sazonov, vainly tried to get the terms of the Austrian ultimatum modified; at the same time, by ordering partial mobilization, he sought to make clear that if Austria attacked Serbia, Russia would act. This calculation misfired for two reasons. First, the news of the partial Russian mobilization did not deter Vienna and Berlin from the course they had charted. Second, the Russian general staff was aghast (it had not been consulted!) for it had no plan for a partial mobilization, so the generals persuaded first Sazonov and then the Tsar that partial mobilization was impracticable and general mobilization inevitable. The Tsar wavered, giving his consent on 29 July and then withdrawing it; but on 30 July he agreed, and on 31 July the order was published.

Russian general mobilization was ordered in the sure knowledge that it would be followed by German mobilization, which, according to the German view, "meant war". In a sense, then, Russia "willed the war", as the Germans were fond of saying; the Italian historian Albertini thinks that the mobilization was premature, for by 30 July Sir Edward Grey had come forward with an idea that might have led to compromise and peace. But inasmuch as Austria had attacked Serbia and Germany had forbidden even the Russian partial mobilization, Russia, as the Russian government saw it, had to mobilize or abdicate as a great power. The Tsar promised that his armies would not attack so long as negotiations continued—but these assurances seemed as flimsy to Germany as the Austrian assurances about the integrity of Serbia did to Russia.

From the beginning of the crisis precipitated by the Austrian ultimatum to Serbia, Germany had declined to restrain its ally and had urged it to act quickly. But by 28 July, the day on which Austria declared war on Serbia, the German Emperor had had a change of heart. Reversing his attitude of 5 July when he urged immediate action, he now sensed that the conciliatory Serbian reply had removed "every reason for war"; he therefore suggested that Austria should stop with the occupation of Belgrade and offer to negotiate. On the following day it began to seem likely that, contrary to German calculations, Britain would be drawn into the war. So the German government shifted its ground and advised Vienna to accept a British proposal, practically identical with that of William II, that after occupying Belgrade, it should offer to negotiate. Before the Austrian government had replied, rumours of Russian mobilization began to reach Berlin. The chief of the general staff, Moltke, now pressed for war (as is admitted by the two most objective German students of the crisis).* On the evening of 30 July he persuaded the chancellor to relax the pressure on Berchtold to accept Grey's proposal, and he himself telegraphed to Conrad urging rejection of this proposal and promising full German support if war resulted. Vienna did as Moltke desired and ordered Austrian general mobilization—before news had been received of the Russian general mobilization.

When the official news of the Russian general mobilization reached Berlin on the morning of 31 July, Moltke, with the help of William II, secured the consent of Bethmann, who had been holding out against the pressure of the generals, to the

* Hermann Lutz, *Die europäische Politik in der Julikrise 1914* (1930), and Alfred von Wegerer, *Der Ausbruch des Weltkrieges* (1939).

proclamation of a " state of danger of war ", which was the necessary preliminary to formal mobilization, the order for which was issued on the following day, 1 August. Whether, without the intervention of Moltke, Austria would have accepted the British proposal, whether a compromise with Russia could have been worked out, no one can say; but it is clear that the interference of Moltke prevented any last-minute attempt to keep the peace.

Because Germany expected to have to fight a two-front war against Russia and France, the general staff had persuaded itself that the only chance of victory lay in a headlong attack on France that was expected to defeat the French in six weeks, after which the German armies would be transferred to the eastern front to meet the more slowly mobilizing Russians. In 1914 there was no plan for an attack first on Russia and a defensive action against France. Yet in 1914 Germany had no quarrel with France. In order to have an excuse for attacking France, the German general staff had to make the Russian mobilization a *casus belli* and then ask France if it would remain neutral; since France would, because of its alliance with Russia, reply in the negative, Germany would then have justification for war against France. But the Prussian minister of war, Falkenhayn, was of the opinion that Germany could wait for several days before responding to the Russian general mobilization; Moltke, however, was so eager for war that the German government did not wait to see if Grey's efforts for peace might be successful.

Germany declared war on Russia on 1 August, which enabled the Russian government to say that it had been attacked while it was ready and anxious to negotiate. The German action required France, according to the Franco-Russian treaty of alliance, to attack Germany, but the French government, in reply to the German ultimatum, instead of replying that it would march with Russia (as expected and desired by Germany), said that it would consult its interests. This reply did not stop the German armies from invading France, and on 3 August Germany declared war on France, alleging, wrongly, that French planes had bombarded Nuremberg. Thus France also appeared to be the victim of brutal aggression, a circumstance of great value to France in consolidating sentiment at home and winning help abroad.

France played little part in the crisis of 1914. It had no direct interest in Serbia, but it was the ally of Russia, and if it did not support Russia in this crisis, the alliance would be broken and France would be left isolated. It happened that at the moment when the Austrian ultimatum was presented in Belgrade, the president of the Republic, Poincaré, and the president of the council of ministers, Viviani, were paying a state visit to Russia, and they gave the Tsar and his ministers the assurance that France would support Russia in resisting Austria-Hungary and Germany, an assurance that certainly strengthened the determination of Sazonov. During the crisis, the French government advised its ally to do nothing that would provide Germany with an excuse for war, but it did not object to any step taken by Russia. This attitude was firmly supported by all shades of French public opinion, and the government did not feel it necessary to reveal the secret terms of the alliance. It will be noted that both Germany and France supported their allies on an issue—Serbia—not of direct concern to themselves, and thus it was that a quarrel between Austria-Hungary and Serbia became transformed, in the interest of the balance of power, into a general European war.

The role of Great Britain was not easy. The crisis found the Liberal government facing the prospect of civil war in Ireland over the question of Home Rule, which may have helped to convince the German government that Britain would remain neutral. Actually, in view of the European situation, the Irish controversy was adjourned, and both the Irish parties supported the government in its efforts to preserve peace. Grey made various proposals for delay, discussion and compromise, all of which were rejected by Austria-Hungary and Germany.

Britain was urged by Germany to accept the principle that the Austro-Serbian conflict should be localized, in other words, to proclaim its neutrality, and by Russia and France to declare its solidarity with them as the only means of stopping Germany from war. Grey, together with the prime minister, Asquith, and some other members of the cabinet, believed that Russia could not be expected to stand aside and abandon Serbia, and Grey, attaching great importance to British relations with Russia, refused to exert pressure on Russia to do so or to advise

Russia against mobilization; they also believed that an Austro-German victory in the approaching struggle would establish a German ascendancy in Europe which would be dangerous for Britain. On the other hand, they could not announce British solidarity with Russia and France because this would have been rejected by the majority of the cabinet and no doubt by both parliament and the country. At the moment, even the limited commitment of 1912 made to France (p. 11) was still secret, as were also the military and naval conversations begun in 1906. Whatever Grey and his group might desire, and they were sure that in its own interests Britain must range itself with France, the temper of the country, at the beginning of the crisis, was predominantly for abstention from the war that seemed likely. Grey privately told the German ambassador that, in the event of war, Britain would be drawn in, but he apparently did not inform the cabinet that he had done so. It was not until Germany had declared war on Russia and sent an ultimatum to France that a promise was given that Britain would defend the northern coast of France against German attack, and even this was made dependent upon the approval of parliament and could be given only because the Conservative opposition promised to support it. As Germany promised not to attack the French coast, the British promise might never have been put to the test had Germany not violated the neutrality of Belgium.

This changed the situation immediately, for the German action persuaded cabinet, parliament and country of the necessity for Britain to join the war. Grey was later reproached for not making clear to Germany much earlier than he did that the violation of Belgium would be a *casus belli*. This would probably have been useless. The German general staff had only *one* plan for fighting the war, a plan which involved going through Belgium, and Moltke was not alarmed by the prospect of British intervention, which he expected; he was confident that his armies would defeat the French before British help arrived or, if the British did manage to land a small army, that it would be easily beaten. It is quite true, as Germans have often asserted, that for Grey the German violation of Belgium was not the reason for British participation in the war, which he advocated on general grounds, but it is equally true that without the Belgian issue, the

24

British government could probably not have persuaded the British people to accept intervention in the war in August 1914.

Ever since 1914 the question has been endlessly debated whether a clear-cut declaration of British solidarity with France and Russia would have prevented the war, but there is no agreement among the publicists, diplomatists and historians who have written on this question. All that can be said with any assurance is that Grey thought it impossible to make such a declaration and never asked it of the cabinet. Mindful of this controversy, the British government of 1939 did make such a declaration, but it did not stop Hitler from making war on Poland.

Italy, the sixth great power, disapproved of the Austrian action from the beginning. In the light of its own history, it did not think it possible for Habsburg power to suppress the Yugoslav national movement by force; but if it did succeed, Italian interests in the Adriatic would be prejudiced. Furthermore, Italy was unwilling to expose its long coastline to the British fleet. The Italian government therefore took advantage of the failure of Austria, in violation of Article VII of the treaty of the Triple Alliance, to inform its ally in advance of its intended action and to arrange compensation, to declare that Germany and Austria were waging a war of aggression and to proclaim its neutrality—which permitted France to withdraw troops from the Italian frontier and send them against Germany.

Previous international crises were long-drawn-out affairs— Morocco 1905, 1911; Near East, 1908–09, 1912–13—during which diplomacy had time to function. In 1914 only thirteen days elapsed from the presentation of the Austrian ultimatum on 23 July to the declaration of war against Germany by Great Britain on 4 August. Austria-Hungary and Germany hoped to force the other powers into accepting their violent programme. To meet this situation, which clearly caught them by surprise, Russia, France and Britain were forced to improvise, with not too happy results. Sazonov and Grey kept making new suggestions almost daily, before their previous proposals had made the rounds of the chanceries and been considered, so that the diplomatic situation grew more and more confused. The confusion reached its height on 1 August, when Germany declared war on Russia, at the very moment when both Austria and Russia seemed at last to be willing to negotiate. A little time was needed to determine what the situation was in fact, but the military men, thinking in terms of mobilization time-tables, had begun to take over from the diplomatists. The three emperors, Francis Joseph, Nicholas II, William II, all hesitated long before they consented to the irrevocable measures of mobilization and declaration of war; unhappily, the first was almost senile, the second a weak character, the third volatile and impetuous. Also, among the numerous men who had to make decisions, there was no out-standing personality—no Cavour, Bismarck or Disraeli—who could dominate the situation.

From 1871 to 1914 the peace of Europe was maintained by the combination of alliances and armaments. In the crises before 1914 governments did not take the plunge because they were not ready for war, were not assured of support from their allies, or did not consider the issue worth fighting for. In 1914 what was at stake was the balance of power in Europe for an indefinite time ahead, and the governments were nearer ready for war than they had been in any previous crisis. Austria-Hungary and Germany insisted on a military solution of the Serbian problem, and clearly wished to upset the *status quo*; Russia, France and Britain were ready to tolerate a diplomatic humiliation of Serbia but not its military subjugation, and while they were not committed to the *status quo*, they were unwilling to see it altered without their consent. Thus the alliances, which had originally served the cause of peace, when put to the final test, almost mechanically operated to convert a local conflict into a general war.

Likewise the great armaments helped to keep the peace—so long as they were not used. But as soon as one power, in order to reinforce its diplomacy, began to mobilize, its action made military men everywhere jittery, for no general staff was willing to allow a rival to get a start. " Once the dice were set rolling," as the German chancellor said, nothing could stop them.

BIBLIOGRAPHY

Since the end of the first world war, many thousands of diplomatic documents have been published from the archives of Austria, France, Germany, Great Britain, Italy and Russia, and the work is still proceeding; the Italian papers begin with 1861, the French and German with 1871, the British with 1898, the Austrian with 1908, the Russian with 1911. The complete files for the crisis of 1914 are said to have been published. There are also innumerable volumes of memoirs by the principal politicians, diplomatists and military men which often supplement the documents.

These materials have been used in hundreds of volumes, of greatly varying quality, by publicists, propagandists and historians; several specialized periodicals, which did not survive the second world war, were devoted to the causes of the first war and the war itself. Practically all of these books were written before the publication of sources was completed, and so they are all " dated ". This is true of the present author's three books on which this pamphlet is based: *Triple Alliance and Triple Entente* (1934), *The Annexation of Bosnia, 1908–1909* (1937), *The Coming of the War 1914* (1930). His article " July 1914: Thirty Years After ", in the *Journal of Modern History*, for September 1944 (reprinted in Herman Ausubel, *The Making of Modern Europe* (1951), II, 942–991) is a condensation of his book on the July crisis revised in the light of later materials.

The reader is therefore referred to two books written since the second world war for the most up-to-date discussion of the years 1871–1914: A. J. P. Taylor, *The Struggle for Mastery in Europe, 1848–1918* (1954), and Pierre Renouvin, *Histoire des Relations Internationales*, Vol. VI, *Le XIXᵉ Siècle: II, De 1871 à 1914, L'Apogée de l'Europe* (1955). Each volume contains a full and critical bibliography, from which students may easily select books in practically all important languages. For the crisis of July 1914 Luigi Albertini, *The Origins of the War of 1914*, Vols. II and III (1953, 1957), replaces all previous accounts; ironically enough, the Italian documents for July 1914 had not been released when Albertini wrote.

THE HISTORIAN'S CONTRIBUTION
TO ANGLO-AMERICAN MISUNDERSTANDING

Report of a committee on National Bias in
Anglo-American History Text Books

ROY ALLEN BILLINGTON

with the collaboration of C P Hill, Angus J Johnston II,
C L Mowat and Charles F Mullett

This examination of text books used in English and American schools
determines the way in which national bias is instilled into school children by
the use of history books. It deals in particular with the treatment of the
American War of Independence, the War of 1812 and World War I. It was
found that there was considerable distortion of British aims and achievements
in American text books. In British text books, however, the treatment of
American history was scant and in one case the American revolution was
dismissed in 12 lines.

ESSAYS ON THIRTEENTH-CENTURY
ENGLAND

The three Presidential Addresses delivered at the Annual Conferences of the
Association by the late Professor R. F. Treharne, with an introductory
appreciation by Glanmor Williams.
Each essay is a valuable contribution in its own right to thirteenth-century
studies. The volume as a whole provides the mature reflections of one of the
leading historians of his day on his own chosen period of English History.

HISTORY AT THE UNIVERSITIES
AND POLYTECHNICS

This fourth edition has been prepared by Mr R. P. Blows and includes
courses at forty universities, and twenty polytechnics and colleges. It also
outlines the Open University courses.

available from the Historical Association

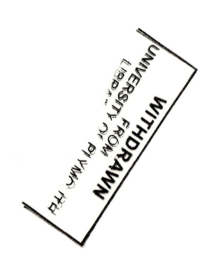